Gabby's Good News

written by SUSAN HARDESTY

illustrated by HECTOR BORLASCA

© 2006 Standard Publishing, Cincinnati, Ohio.
A division of Standex International Corporation. All rights reserved.
Printed in the United States of America.
Series design: Robert Glover. Cover and interior design: Steve Clark.

ISBN 0-7847-1928-4

12 11 10 09 08 07 06   9 8 7 6 5 4 3 2 1

Standard®
PUBLISHING
Bringing The Word to Life

Cincinnati, Ohio

Gabby's Mom woke her up early.

"Good morning! Time to get up for school!"

Gabby rubbed her eyes sleepily and dragged herself out of bed.

She slowly dressed in the clothes her mom had set out.

By the time Gabby came downstairs for breakfast, her dad was already at the table.

"Why do you always read the paper?" Gabby asked.

"I want to know the news," her father answered.

He looked at Gabby. "You know some *very* good news."

"I do?" asked Gabby.

"Yes! You know the good news we read about in the Bible, the news of God's love," he said. "The news in the paper can't compare. God's love is worth telling everyone about!"

Gabby finished her breakfast, brushed her teeth, and hugged her mom good-bye. She followed her dad outside. The bus for school was already waiting for her. She waved good-bye to her dad and quickly got on the bus.

Today Gabby noticed there was a new kid on the bus.
No one else was sitting by him so she did.

"Hello! My name is Gabby. Are you new here?" she asked.

"Hi, I'm Luis. My family just moved here from
Mexico," Luis smiled shyly.

Gabby was nervous. She didn't know what to say.

As the bus pulled up to the school, Gabby remembered her dad saying she had some good news to tell.

"Would you like to hear my special news?" Gabby asked as they got off the bus.

"Yes!" said Luis. "What is your special news?"

"My news is the best news ever, that God loves all of us very much!" Gabby said. "If you want, you can go to church with my family. My teacher, Ms. Kathy, tells us stories from the Bible about God's love and about his Son, Jesus."

Luis promised to ask his mom when he got home from school. Gabby opened the door for Luis. She said a little prayer in her mind, asking God to help Luis be able to come to church with her on Sunday.

Gabby helped Luis find the school's office and then made her way to her own class. All morning long she thought about how good it felt to tell Luis her good news. She hoped she would get to tell someone else her good news!

When it was time for recess, Gabby played with her best friends, Ashley and Ella. Ashley looked a little sad so Gabby asked her what was wrong.

Ashley started crying, "My cat is missing! She didn't show up for dinner last night!"

"Well I have some good news that might help," said Gabby. "I read in my Bible that God loves us so much and we can talk to him anytime."

"Do you think God cares about my cat?" asked Ashley.

"I know God cares," said Gabby. She started praying. "God, thank you for loving Ashley. Please help her cat, Prissy, find her way home. Please help Ashley not worry. Amen."

Then the whistle blew and the friends ran to get in line.

"Thanks, Gabby," Ashley said. "It makes me feel better to know that God loves me."

"Me, too!" said Ella.

Gabby was so glad. They all felt better! They didn't even worry about their math test coming up!

When the bus stopped at her house, Gabby got off so quickly she forgot to wave to her friends. She was in a hurry to get inside the house and tell her mom about her exciting day. But her mom was busy cooking supper, so Gabby worked quietly on her homework. Then she set the table for supper, hoping her dad would come home soon.

Finally, her dad came home and they all sat down for dinner. Her dad prayed, thanking God for food to eat. As soon as he said, "Amen," Gabby couldn't hold it in any longer.

"Mom! Dad! I told the good news to two people today!" said Gabby. She told them about Luis and Ashley and sharing God's love with them.

"That certainly is great news!" smiled her mom. "I am so proud of you."

"Me, too!" said her dad. "I hope Luis can go to church with us on Sunday."

Before climbing into bed that night, Gabby stopped to pray.

"Thank you, God, for the good news of your love! Thank you for the chance to tell others about Jesus! Please help me to remember to tell your news to others. Amen."